THE INEVITABLE FORCES OF AN IMMINENT & UNEXPECTED CHANGE

If a man die, shall he live again? All the days of my appointed time will I wait, till my change come.

Job 14:14

by

Franklin N. Abazie

The Inevitable Forces of an Imminent & Expected Change
COPYRIGHT 2017 BY Franklin N Abazie
ISBN: 978-0-996626-36-1

All right reserved. This book or any portion thereof may not be reproduced or used in any manner whatsoever without the express written permission of the publisher, except for the use of brief quotations in a book review. All Bible quotes are from King James Version and others as noted.

Published by: F N ABAZIE PUBLISHING HOUSE- aka, Empowerment Bookstore.

That I may publish with the voice of thanksgiving and tell of all thy wondrous works.
Psalms 26:7

To order additional copies, wholesales or booking:
Call the Church office (973-372-7518),
or Empowerment Bookstore Hotline (973-393-8518)

Worship address:
343 Sanford Avenue Newark New Jersey 07106
Administrative Head Office address:
33 Schley Street Newark New Jersey 07112
Email:pastorfranknto@yahoo.com
Website www.fnabaziehealingministries.org
Publishing House: www.fnabaziepublishinghouse.org

This book is a production of F N Abazie Publishing House.
A publication Arms of Miracle of God Ministries 2017.
First Edition

CONTENTS

THE MANDATE OF THE COMMISSION iv

ARMS OF THE COMMISSION v

INTRODUCTION vi

CHAPTER 1
1 The Dawning of a New Day..................... 1

CHAPTER 2
2 Overcoming The Foces of Setbacks 11

CHAPTER 3
3 Prayer of Salvation................................. 61

CHAPTER 4
4 About The Author................................... 70

THE MANDATE OF THE COMMISSION

"The moment is due to impact your world through the revival of the healing & miracle ministry of Jesus Christ of Nazareth."

"I am sending you to restore health unto thee and I will heal thee of thy wounds, said the Lord of Host."

ARMS OF THE COMMISSION

1) F N Abazie Ministries-Miracle of God Ministries (Miracle Chapel Intl)

2) F N Abazie TV Ministries: Global Television Ministry Outreach

3) F N Abazie Radio Ministries: Radio Broadcasting Outreach

4) F N Abazie Publishing House: Book Publication

5) F N Abazie Bible School: also called Word of Healing Bible School (W.O.H.B.S)

6) F N Abazie Evangelistic Ass: Miracle of God Ministries: Global Crusade

7) Empowerment Bookstore: Book distribution

8) F N Abazie Helping Hands: Meeting the help of the needy world wide

9) F N Abazie Disaster Recovery Mission: Global Disaster Recovery

10) F N Abazie Prison Ministry: Prison Ministry for all convicts "Second chance"

Some of our ministry arms are waiting the appointed time to commence.

FAVOR CONFESSION

Father thank you for making me righteous and accepted through the blood of Jesus Christ. Because of that, I am blessed and highly favored by God. I am the subject of your affection. Your favor surrounds me as a shield, and the first thing that people see around me is your favored shield. Thank you that I have favor with you and man today. All day long people go out of their way to bless me and help me. I have favor with everyone that I deal with today. Doors that were once closed are now opened for me. I receive preferential treatment, and I have special privileges, I am Gods favored child.

No good thing will he withhold from me. Because of Gods favor my enemies cannot triumph over my life. I have supernatural increase and promotion. I declare restoration to everything that the devil has stolen from my life. I have honor in the midst of my adversaries and an increase in assets, especially in real estate and expansion of territories.

Because I am highly favored by God, I experience great victories, supernatural turnarounds, and miraculous breakthrough in the midst of great impossibilities. I receive recognition, prominence, and honor. Petitions are granted to me even by ungodly authorities. Policies, rules, regulations, and laws are changed and reverse on my behalf.

I win battles that I don't even have to fight, because God fights them for me. This is the day, the set time and the designated moment for me to experience the free favor of God, that profusely and lavishly abound on my behalf in Jesus name. Amen.

INTRODUCTION

"When thou goest out to battle against thine enemies, and seest horses, and chariots, and a people more than thou, be not afraid of them: for the Lord thy God is with thee, which brought thee up out of the land of Egypt."
Duet 20:1

This book is a guide to anyone experiencing any form of *inevitable & un-expected-imminent change in life*. Changes in life are real and certain; we must embrace every change in life with an attitude of gratitude. Although *"nothing lasts forever"*. We must learn to appreciate believe and trust God to help us overcome in whatever prevailing situation we find ourselves. President Obama once said and I quote, *"Change will not come if we wait for some other person or some other time. We are the ones we've been waiting for. We are the change that we seek."*

In my own opinion we must constantly, and consciously be open to change in life. There are some *positive breakthrough* changes in life that we admire, and desire to attain in life. *There are also other prevailing, and imminent changes in life that forces quite a few of us to settle for less in life. For example, death of a love one, sickness, injury, disease, divorce, mental sickness, depression, e.t.c.*

For the most part, most of us live in denial. Until we accept the reality, we will forever deceive ourselves. This publication is a guide for anyone living in denial, or anyone who had experienced setbacks in life.

"But we all, with open face beholding as in a glass the glory of the Lord, are changed into the same image from glory to glory, even as by the Spirit of the Lord." **2 Cor 3:18**

Changes, by definition, are the building blocks of life. Although God is love, *God is also a God is change and season. "And he changeth the times and the seasons: he removeth kings, and setteth up kings: he giveth wisdom unto the wise, and knowledge to them that know understanding."* **Daniel 2:21**

This publication is a comfort guide to anyone going through depression, sickness and disease, injury, divorce, mental sickness of any kind, fear, e.t.c. We are told, *"For there is hope of a tree, if it be cut down, that it will sprout again, and that the tender branch thereof will not cease."* **Job 14:7**

Often we live in denial, unless we accept the truth of God's word, we will forever live in denial. We are told, *"And ye shall know the truth, and the truth shall make you free."* (John 8:32) *May this book be of help to you in the mighty Name of Jesus. Amen*

HIS DESTINY WAS THE **CROSS**....

HIS PURPOSE WAS **LOVE**.....

HIS REASON WAS **YOU**....

"And ye shall know the truth, and the truth shall make you free."

John 8:32

"For we can do nothing against the truth, but for the truth."

2 Cor 13:8

"If a man die, shall he live again? all the days of my appointed time will I wait, till my change come."

Job 14:14

CHANGE BY FIRE PRAYER POINTS

"If a man die, shall he live again? All the days of my appointed time will I wait, till my change come..."
Job 14:14

I declare NEVER AGAIN! To any bad experience I have had in my life, it shall not repeat itself, in the name of Jesus.

I come against repeated oppression in the Name of Jesus.

I come against any family strong man, in the name of Jesus.

I destroy repeated calamities in the Mighty Name of Jesus.

AFFLICTION! Hear the word of the Lord, NEVER AGAIN will you rise!!! In the name of Jesus.

Witchcraft manipulations, NEVER AGAIN! in the name of Jesus.

Demonic powers assigned to use me as foot mat, I cry against you, NEVER AGAIN! In the name of Jesus.

The power behind 'almost there', I cry against you, NEVER AGAIN! In the name of Jesus.

Spirit of confusion, I cry against you, NEVER AGAIN! In the name of Jesus.

Powers closing my heavens, I cry against you, NEVER AGAIN! In the name of Jesus.

Spirit of stagnation, assigned against my life, I cry against you, NEVER AGAIN! In the name of Jesus.

Access of darkness into my life, TERMINATE BY FIRE! In the name of Jesus.

The lions of past problems roaring against me, SHUT UP! BE SILENCED!! In the name of Jesus.

Shame and disfavor, I cry against you, NEVER AGAIN! In the name of Jesus.

Diminishing returns, I cry against you, NEVER AGAIN! In the name of Jesus.

Visitations of the merchants of death, DIE!!! In the name of Jesus.

Satanic embarrassments, I cry against you, NEVER AGAIN! In the name of Jesus.

EVERYTHING, hear the word of the Lord, TURN AROUND FOR MY FAVOUR!!! In the name of Jesus.

I dismantle every strong hold designed to imprison my talent in the mighty name of Jesus.

I reject every cycle of frustration, in the name of Jesus.

Power of God paralyze every agent assigned to frustrate my life in the name of Jesus.

Finger of God, grant me supernatural speed against all my contenders in the name of Jesus.

By the blood of Jesus, I destroy every familiar spirit caging my life and career.

Fire of God arrest every demonic agents, assigned to police my destiny and marriage.

By the blood of Jesus, I proclaim no weapon fashioned against me shall ever prosper.

Holy Spirit of God break me through and forward in life in the mighty name of Jesus.

God, smash me and renew my strength, in the name of Jesus.

Holy Spirit, open my eyes to see beyond the visible to the invisible, in the name of Jesus.

Father Lord grant me strength and power in the name of Jesus.

O Lord, liberate my spirit to follow the leading of the Holy Spirit.

Holy Spirit, teach me to pray through problems instead of praying about, it in the name of Jesus.

Father Lord, deliver me from the false accusation in life, in the name of Jesus.

By the blood of Jesus, every evil spiritual padlock and evil chain hindering my success, be roasted, in the name of Jesus.

By the blood of Jesus I rebuke every spirit of spiritual deafness and blindness in my life, in the name of Jesus.

Father Lord, empower me to dominate the enemy of my destiny in the name of Jesus.

Jesus Christ of Nazareth, heal my infirmities in the name of Jesus

Lord, anoint my eyes and my ears that they may see and hear wondrous things from heaven.

Father Lord, anoint me with power and authority to dominate all my enemies in the name of Jesus.

Fire of God roast every giant rising up against my life and career.

Holy Spirit of God destroy all my oppressors in the name of Jesus.

Angels of good new, bring my good news to me in the mighty name of Jesus.

Every strong man holding me down, lose your hold now in the name of Jesus.

I nullify every demonic prediction over my life in the name of Jesus.

By the blood of Jesus, I flush out every polluted deposit of the enemy in my life.

By the blood of Jesus, I paralyze every enemy of my promotion in the name of Jesus.

Father Lord, destroy any power tormenting my life that is not from you.

Holy Ghost fire, ignite the fire of revival in my life.

By the blood of Jesus, I declare victory over every conflicting trial.

By the Blood of Jesus, I command the arrest of every demonic spirit, militating against my life.

By the blood of Jesus, I proclaimed the blood of Jesus, over every device of the enemy.

By the blood of Jesus, I revoke stagnation and hardship over my life in the name of Jesus.

Holy Ghost fire, destroy every satanic arrangement in my life, in the name of Jesus.

CHAPTER 1

THE DAWNING OF A NEW DAY

"Be strong and of a good courage, fear not, nor be afraid of them: for the Lord thy God, he it is that doth go with thee; he will not fail thee, nor forsake thee."
Deuteronomy 31:6

Although there are several relevant definitions of breakthrough in life, *I define breakthrough in life, simply as the breaking of a new day.* Every day that you wake up in the morning, *you should thank God for that day.* A lot of folks slept and died in their sleep. David said, *"I laid me down and slept; I awaked; for the Lord sustained me."* Psalms 3:5

The dawning of a new day to me means witnessing the change you long desire in life. *There is nothing God cannot do for us in life, if only we can believe and trust in Him. "Jesus said unto him, If thou canst believe, all things are possible to him that believeth."* (Mark 9:23) If you have been experience setback and prevailing challenges in life, there is a day with the Lord to end it all. Jesus Christ put it this way. *"...for the things concerning me have an end."* (Luke 22:37) If only we can trust God and *believe in*

Him, there is an end to that challenge, there is a stop to that obstacle, there is an end to that sickness and disease.

We are told by the Holy Scripture that, *"Hope deferred maketh the heart sick: but when the desire cometh, it is a tree of life."* (Proverb 13:12) If we must experience the dawning of a new day, then we must be courageous, bold, fearless, and faithful. God said to Joshua, *"Every place that the sole of your foot shall tread upon, that have I given unto you, as I said unto Moses."* Joshua 1:3

What does it mean to experience a change in life?

The American Heritage college dictionary defines a changes as follows: *Change means to cause to be different, to give a completely different form or appearance to; transform. To give and receive reciprocally; interchange. To exchange for or replace with another usually of the same category. To lay aside, abandon, or leave for another; Switch: change sides. To put a fresh covering on-To become different or undergo alteration. To undergo transformation or transition.*

President John F Kennedy once said, *"Change is the law of life. And those who look only to the past or present are certain to miss the future."*

Jeff Bezos once said....

"What we need to do is always lean into the future; when the world changes around you and when it changes against you - what used to be a tail wind is now a head wind - you have to lean into that and figure out what to do because complaining isn't a strategy."

It is written, *"I am the Lord I change not therefore ye sons of Jacob are not consumed."* Malachi 3:6

Unless we believe and trust God for the desired change in our finances, marriage, career, e.t.c. in life, we forever live in frustration. Often most folks get easily frustrated in times of difficulties and hardship. May I submit to you that *"every season is for a while and not forever."* It is written, *"For our light affliction, which is but for a moment, worketh for us a far more exceeding and eternal weight of glory."* 2 Cor 4:17

In my opinion, nothing last forever. Jesus made a profound statement concerning Himself. *"For the things concerning me have an end."* Every season is for a while. Every challenge is for a moment.

Unless we focus on the desired change we want to see in life, we deceive ourselves. Everyone must be realistic to themselves otherwise we deceive ourselves. Perhaps you lost a job that is not the reason you should end up in a mental home. Perhaps you lost your money that is not enough reason to become suicidal or turn to alcohol or drugs. Every believer must turn to God in all times. Not only in times of trouble but also in times of peace and prosperity.

A graphic example of someone who overcame unbelievable hardship is "Job." It is recorded that for nine months job suffered total collapse of his business and land properties. At one point Job's wife advised him to curse God and die. It is written, "But he knoweth the way that I take: when he hath tried me, I shall come forth as gold." Job 23:10

Often there certain changes that will take almost a life time to enforce. There are some of us that will rather die than live in certain circumstances. I read a story of Nelson Mandela, who was willing to perish in prison than suffer Apartheid in South Africa. Mahatma Gandhi once said, *"You must be the change you wish to see in the world."*

If I am permitted to put this way, if anything new must happen to us, we must initiate it, and be willing to execute it to the end. If you must change your finance, you must plan, prepare, and do the same things successful people do daily. In my opinion, just a daily change in the things we do, will go a long way to affect our life positively. It takes will power by the Spirit of God to effect any desired change in life. It is written, "Arise ye, and depart; for this is not your rest: because it is polluted, it shall destroy you, even with a sore destruction." Micah 2:10

CHANGE YOUR HEART

It is written, "For as he thinketh in his heart, so is he: Eat and drink, saith he to thee; but his heart is not with thee." **Proverb 23:7**

For the most part, unless we change the way we think we are not entitled to experience the manifestation of the changes that we expect in life. One man said, "as you lay your bed, so will you lie on it." In my own opinion, I believe life to be practical and not mystical.

You are responsible to the outcome of your life. We are told "And be not conformed to this world: but be ye transformed by the renewing of your mind, that ye may prove what is that good, and acceptable, and perfect, will of God." Romans 12:2

Until we change the way we think, we cannot experience the change that we desire in life. Although most people tend to blames others for their failure in life in my opinion, everyone is absolutely responsible for the outcome of their lives. We must change the way we think, the way we live, and the way we deal with everyone and everything around us. "For in him we live, and move, and have our being; as certain also of your own poets have said, for we are also his offspring." Acts 17:26

George Bernard Shaw once said, *"Progress is impossible without change, and those who cannot change their minds cannot change anything."* Most changes in life begin from our heart. Our heart produce our words, our words define our action. Our actions further develop our habits, and our habits define our character, and our character produces our lifestyle. We were warned, "Keep thy heart with all diligence; for out of it are the issues of life." (Proverb 4:23) No man can make our personal changes in life for us. It is written, "Now the Lord is that Spirit: and where the Spirit of the Lord is, there is liberty." 2 Cor 3:17

HOW DO I PROVOKE THE DAWNING OF A NEW DAY?

~CALL ON THE NAME OF JESUS

None of us is permitted to experience the dawning of a new day, *unless we have the access key by calling on the Name of Jesus in faith in times of prevailing drastic changes or perhaps in times of desired changes in life.*

~PRAYER IN FAITH

Jesus told us that challenges will come in this world. Unless we develop the spirit to pray in faith for a supernatural encounter, we will never experience the dawning of a new day (breakthrough in life).

~PERSISTANT PRAYER

Unless we develop the spirit to pray often and with the spirit of persistent, we will never prevail in life. If you must overcome your present obstacle, then you must bombard the kingdom of Heaven with strong violent but persistent prayers daily.

~FASTING & PRAYER

If I may say it this way, nothing changes for us all unless we pray consistently and fast as often. It is written, *"Howbeit this kind goeth not out but by prayer and fasting."* (Matthew 17:21) There are some force that unless we pray constantly with perseverance, we will never prevail against that obstacle in life.

~PRAY ACCORDING TO THE WILL OF THE FATHER

It is written, *"Thy kingdom come, Thy will be done in earth, as it is in heaven."* (Matthew 6:10) We must always pray kingdom oriented prayer. We must pray for ourselves and for others, otherwise we become self-centered and God hates selfish self-centered people.

~BE STILL IN LIFE

Every time we really want a change in our life, we must let the Spirit of God lead and direct us. If you are not still the Spirit cannot help you. It is written, "For the Lord shall rise up as in mount Perazim, he shall be wroth as in the valley of Gibeon, that he may do his work, his strange work; and bring to pass his act, his strange act." Isaiah 28:21

As long as you invited God to intervene over that prevailing challenge in your life, we must be still and let God work. It is written, "Be still, and know that I am God: I will be exalted among the heathen, I will be exalted in the earth." Psalms 46:10

~PATIENCE IN LIFE

Often, most of us are in hurry, especially when the desire is not forth coming in life. God will allow us to wait for the best job, career, connection, e.t.c in life, because Jesus always reserve the best at the last moment. I once heard a saying that the *"patient dog eats the fattest bone."* Patience is all it takes if we must experience a new season in life. It is written, *"Cast not away therefore your confidence, which hath great recompence of reward. For ye have need of patience, that, after ye have done the will of God, ye might receive the promise."* Hebrews 10:35-36

~LEARN TO FORGIVE OTHERS

Most folks live in bitterness. It is written, *"For if ye forgive men their trespasses, your heavenly Father will also forgive you: But if ye forgive not men their trespasses, neither will your Father forgive your trespasses."* (Matthew 6:14-15) If you must experience breakthrough in life, you must learn to live in forgives with everyone around you. Living in forgiveness provokes breakthrough in life. Whenever you live in forgives, you live in freedom. I once heard one of my uncles say that *"to err is human, but to forgive is divine."* Forgiveness in life is a mystery of the Kingdom of God. If we must breakthrough in life, we must practice forgiving others as a lifestyle.

~WE MUST REPENT OUR SINS

Unless we repent of our sins, we are not ready for deliverance. Repentance is the first key into deliverance in life. If you must become great you must embrace repentance and humility in life. We must ask God in prayers to forgive us our trespasses in life. It is written, "For all have sinned, and come short of the glory of God." Romans 3:23

CHAPTER 2

DOMINATING THE FORCES OF SETBACKS

"Have not I commanded thee? Be strong and of a good courage; be not afraid, neither be thou dismayed: for the Lord thy God is with thee whithersoever thou goest."
Joshua 1:9

There *are forces that are designed to set us back in life. For example divorce, sickness, disease, injury, adultery, drug abuse, alcohol abuse e.t.c. These are just a few example of setback forces that can keep anyone depressed in life. So many great men and women are depressed and sick today, because of these prevailing forces of obstacles.* May I submit to you that anyone can overcome setback in life. These forces have power to dominate anyone, *"only if you permit it to happen to you."* It is written, *"For sin shall not have dominion over you: for ye are not under the law, but under grace."* Romans 6:14

Despite what may be going through in life, God is able to deliver you from it all. There is a way out for you, there is a way up for you, and there is a way forward for you in life. The book of Nahum posed a unique question about God. It is written, *"What do ye imagine against the Lord? He will make an utter end: affliction shall not rise up the second time."* Nahum 1:9

Unless we discharge the devil, we will yield the victory to the enemy. Although there are forces of an imminent change in life, we must consciously believe God to dominate any prevailing change against us in life. It is written, "Fear thou not; for I am with thee: be not dismayed; for I am thy God: I will strengthen thee; yea, I will help thee; yea, I will uphold thee with the right hand of my righteousness." Isaiah 41:10

ALWAYS PUT YOUR HOPE AND TRUST IN THE LORD

Often some fellows put their trust and hope in a man. The bible warned us not to trust in any man. We were told, *"Thus saith the Lord; Cursed be the man that trusteth in man, and maketh flesh his arm, and whose heart departeth from the Lord. For he shall be like the heath in the desert, and shall not see when good cometh; but shall inhabit the parched places in the wilderness, in a salt land and not inhabited."* Jer 17:5-6

May nobody fool you, everybody is going through something in life. May I suggest to you, not to live in denial. What so ever you are experiencing as a change in your life, I love you to be realistic and accept the truth about it. It is compulsory that you place your trust and confidence in the Lord your God. It is written, "My soul, wait thou only upon God; for my expectation is from him". (Psalms 62:5) Every time you are going through any prevailing obstacle in life, I believe it is not the right time for us to place our confidence in anyone. It is written, *"Confidence in an unfaithful man in time of trouble is like a broken tooth, and a foot out of joint."* Proverb 25:19

GOD IS A GOD OF SEASON AND TIME

Often most of us get very religious, and delusional. The truth is we must be honest and realistic especially to ourselves. There is a time and a season over your life. I do not know the season you are experiencing in your life but we were told, *"Cast not away therefore your confidence, which hath great recompence of reward. For ye have need of patience, that, after ye have done the will of God, ye might receive the promise."* Hebrews 10:35-36

THERE IS AN END TO EVERY SEASON IN YOUR LIFE

We all have our own season to shine and arise. Often no one wants the season to suffer hunger and lack. We all look forward to our blessing season in life. It is written, "To everything there is a season, and a time to every purpose under the heaven: A time to be born, and a time to die; a time to plant, and a time to pluck up that which is planted; A time to kill, and a time to heal; a time to break down, and a time to build up; A time to weep, and a time to laugh; a time to mourn, and a time to dance; A time to cast away stones, and a time to gather stones together; a time to embrace, and a time to refrain from embracing; A time to get, and a time to lose; a time to keep, and a time to cast away; A time to rend, and a time to sew; a time to keep silence, and a time to speak; A time to love, and a time to hate; a time of war, and a time of peace. What profit hath he that worketh in that wherein he laboureth? I have seen the travail, which God hath given to the sons of men to be exercised in it." Eccl3:1-10.

If I may ask you, when was the last time you experienced challenges in your life — We are talking of those prevailing times when you needed help and comfort from anyone. When you lost your confidence, and all you wanted to do was to cry like a baby. The truth is that at some point in life, we all go through frustration, difficulty and struggle in one area of our life or the other.

Often we *all respond differently to adversities. As believer of the gospel of Jesus*

Christ we have an overcoming power in the blood of Jesus to dominate any prevailing hardship or adverse condition in life. Every successful Christian alive today is a testament to the infinite power of God.

HOW DO I OVERCOME SETBACKS IN LIFE?

FAITH IN GOD

We were told that *"without faith we cannot please God."* If God must change your season then you must be faithful in your personal life. The bible said, *"..weeping may endure for a night, but joy cometh in the morning."* (Psalms 30:5) Faith in God is the foundation to overcome any form of setback in life.

BELIEVE IN YOUR SELF

We must believe in our own ability to launch a comeback. Unless you believe in your potential no one else will believe in you. If you must overcome this season of your life, you must believe in yourself and develop self-confidence in what you can accomplish in life.

SELF CONFIDENCE AND MOTIVATION

If we must overcome prevailing season in our lives, we must remain inspired with the word of God. God's promises are true, we were told. *The scripture can never be broken.*

BELIEVE GOD

Unless we believe in God, we make His word a lie. We must believe the word of God, believe in God to see us through any prevailing predicament in life.

MAKE THE PROGRESSIVE CHANGES TOWARDS THE DESIRED FUTURE

We must make the progressive changes towards the desired future. No man arrives at a future suddenly. *Like Zig Ziglar said and I quote, we are born to win, but for us to win, we must plans to succeed, prepare to succeed and expect we will succeed. Albert Einstein once said, and I quote, that is insanity to do the same thing over and over, and expect a different result.*

ENDURANCE IN TIMES OF DIFFICULTIES

Unless we develop the spirit of endurance in time of trouble, we make our faith confession fake. We must develop the skills to overcome challenges and obstacles in life. It is written, *"For whatsoever is born of God overcometh the world: and this is the victory that overcometh the world, even our faith. Who is he that overcometh the world, but he that believeth that Jesus is the Son of God?"* 1 John 5:4-5

WE MUST BE OPEN MINDED TO ACCEPT THE REALITY

Often we live in denial, but unless we accept the reality we deceive ourselves in life. For the most part, accepting the truth is a good cause for action. You may ask me how about if this is a change I couldn't control? Well, that's is what I am talking about.

BE STRATEGIC TO OVERCOME CHALLENGES

In my opinion to be strategic means to develop an action plan, and to execute that plan to the end. Most of us only pray, and fold our hands, expecting God to come down to help us. If God must help you, then you must be strategic and proactive in all things. It is written, "The desire accomplished is sweet to the soul:.." Proverb 13:19

HINDRANCES TO CHANGE IN LIFE

~DESPERATION

Every time you are in a hurry, you disqualify yourself from the blessings of God. Desperation hinders the mystery of hope in God from validation. Often most folks say, I hope in God but they are in a rush and cannot wait for something good to happen. It is written, *"he that believeth shall not make haste."* Isaiah 28:16

We are certain to miss out on our blessing every time we are in a rush and desperate. Have you forgotten? *"Do not be anxious about anything, but in every situation, by prayer and petition, with thanksgiving, present your requests to God."* (Phil 4:6) In my own opinion desperation proves that we lack of faith in God. If we must hope in God, we must not be desperate. If faith in God must work for us, we must not be in a hurry.

~GREEDINESS & COVETOUSNESS

It's difficult to admit to greediness, but most of us are greedy to a high degree. God hates greedy people. We are told, "And he said unto them, Take heed, and beware of covetousness: for a man's life consisteth not in the abundance of the things which he possesseth." (Luke 12:15) Most greedy people build their faith in fake hope. The truth is they build their hope in material things that have no genuine value in life. Recall. "But godliness with contentment is great gain"

It is written, *"Lay not up for yourselves treasures upon earth, where moth and rust doth corrupt, and where thieves break through and steal: But lay up for yourselves treasures in heaven, where neither moth nor rust doth corrupt, and where thieves do not break through nor steal."* Matthew 6:19-20

~ SIN IN OUR LIFE

Unless we deal with the old man of sin. We will never see true light in Christ. Unless we deal with sin in our lives, we will never experience genuine salvation in Christ. We are told, "Wherefore he saith, Awake thou that sleepest, and arise from the dead, and Christ shall give thee light." Ephesians 5:14

Unless we appear pure before Him, our

hope in him is fake. It is written blessed are the pure in heart "Blessed are the pure in heart: for they shall see God." (Matthew 5:8). Unless we genuinely deal with sin our hope in God is fake. We are told, *"Now we know that God heareth not sinners: but if any man be a worshipper of God, and doeth his will, him he heareth."*

Sin erodes destiny. It decays our glorious path. Remember..."*the path of a just man is like a shining light.."* (Proverb 4:18) *"If we confess our sins, he is faithful and just to forgive us our sins, and to cleanse us from all unrighteousness."* (1 John 1:9) Sin is one of the strongest forces that will stop any one from hoping genuinely in God.

~PRIDE

Although they acclaim to hope in God, but most proud men/women do not genuinely hope in God. We are told that *God hates a proud look, a lying tongue, and hands that shed innocent blood.* If we claim to hope in God we must humble ourselves before him. Eventually, God will exalt us in due time. *"Humble yourselves therefore under the mighty hand of God, that he may exalt you in due time."* (1 Peter 5:6) Pride hinders hope in God. *Pride goeth before destruction, and an haughty spirit before a fall.* Proverb 16:18

ACCESS INTO THE SUPERNATURAL

WALKING IN THE SPIRIT:

Unless we obey scriptural command we shall never operate in the supernatural. Every time we walk in the spirit we cheaply have access into the supernatural realm. In my opinion walking in the Spirit is the gateway into riches and abundance of wealth in Christ Jesus. *"But the natural man receiveth not the things of the Spirit of God: for they are foolishness unto him: neither can he know them, because they are spiritually discerned."* 1 Cor 2:14

Remember....

"This I say then, Walk in the Spirit, and ye shall not fulfil the lust of the flesh." Gal 5:17

BORN AGAIN

However it may sound, we must hear it again. We must be born again. *"But the natural man receiveth not the things of the Spirit of God: for they are foolishness unto him: neither can he know them, because they are spiritually discerned."* If you are not born again, you are missing out on the blessings of God. For us to access the blessings of the Lord, we must genuinely repent of our sins. *"Jesus answered and said unto him, Verily, verily, I say unto thee, except a man be born again, he cannot see the kingdom of God."* John 3:3

Born again status grants us access to unlimited riches of His glory. We must make plans to make heaven if we are genuinely serving God. Eternity is real so make your own plan to make heaven by being born again.

FAITH IN GOD

Faith in God is the platform to operate in the supernatural. Faith in God is the gateway for His unlimited riches. Faith in God is the breathing grounds for hope in God to validate. Unless there is faith in God our hope is fake. *"For we are saved by hope: but hope that is seen is not hope: for what a man seeth, why doth he yet hope for?"* Romans 8:24

For anyone to access the supernatural we must have genuine faith in God and in His word. *"And Jesus answering saith unto them, Have faith in God."* (Mark 11:22) *"We having the same spirit of faith, according as it is written, I believed, and therefore have I spoken; we also believe, and therefore speak."* 2 Cor 4:13

WALK IN AGREEMENT

It is commanded to walk in agreement with the Holy Spirit. It is the will of God to walk according to the leading of the Holy Spirit. For no man can walk with God and fail in life. *"Can two walk together, except they both agreed?"* (Amos3:3) For us to experience great things in life we must walk in agreement and in the spirit.

WALKING IN LOVE

It is written, *"but faith which worketh by love."* Walking in love grants us access into the deep things of God. We are told, *"But as it is written, Eye hath not seen, nor ear heard, neither have entered into the heart of man, the things which God hath prepared for them that love him."* 1 Cor 2:9

Walking in love grants us the unlimited access into His glory. *"And we have known and believed the love that God hath to us. God is love; and he that dwelleth in love dwelleth in God, and God in him."* 1 John 4:16

WALKING IN TRUTH

Often we lie to our friends, to ourselves, and to God, but until you tell yourself the truth, you are not ready to experience and access the supernatural. Walking in truth in light and command of the scripture is the breathing ground for encounter with the supernatural. For unless we tell ourselves the truth we are not ready to experience the power of His majesty. We are told, *"For we can do nothing against the truth, but for the truth."* 2 Cor 13:8

Unless you embrace, and engraft the truth into your own life, we will forever remain in want of all things. We must accept the truth and release ourselves from the shackles of deceit, fraud, malice, envy, strive, fornication adultery e.t.c. *"If the Son therefore shall make you free, ye shall be free indeed."* John 8:32

PRAYER POINTS THAT WORK

I cancel my name and that of my family from the death register, with the fire of God, in the name of Jesus.

Every weapon of destruction fashioned against me and my family, be destroyed by the fire of God, in the name of Jesus.

Power of God, fight for me in every area of my life, in Jesus' name.

Every hindrance to my breakthrough, be melted by the fire of God, in the name of Jesus.

Every evil power against me, be scattered by the thunder fire of God, in the name of Jesus.

Father Lord, destroy every evil man/woman in the name of Jesus.

Every failures of the past, be converted to success, in Jesus' name.

Father Lord, let the former rain, the latter rain and Your blessing pour down on me now.

Father Lord, let all the failure turn into success for me, in the name of Jesus.

I receive power from on high and I paralyze all the powers of darkness that are diverting my blessings, in the name of Jesus.

Beginning from this day, I employ the services of the angels of God to open unto me every door of opportunity and breakthroughs, in the name of Jesus.

I will not go around in circles again, I will make progress, in the name of Jesus.

I shall not build for another to inhabit and I shall not plant for another to eat, in the name of Jesus.

I paralyse the powers of the emptier concerning my handiwork, in the name of Jesus.

O Lord, let every locust, caterpillar and palmerworm assigned to eat the fruit of my labour be roasted by the fire of God.

The enemy shall not spoil my testimony in this programme, in the name of Jesus.

By the blood of Jesus, I reject every backward journey, in the name of Jesus.

By the blood of Jesus, I paralyze every strongman attached to any area of my life, in the name of Jesus.

I pray, Let every agent of shame fashioned to work against my life be paralyzed, in the name of Jesus.

I paralyse the activities of household wickedness over my life, in the name of Jesus.

I quench every strange fire emanating from evil tongues against me, in the name of Jesus.

Father Lord, give me power for maximum achievement.

Heavenly father, give me comforting authority to achieve my goal.

Blood of Jesus Christ, defend and fortify me with Your power.

I paralyse every spirit of disobedience in my life, in Jesus' name.

I refuse to disobey the voice of God, in the name of Jesus.

Every root of rebellion in my life, be uprooted, in Jesus' name.

By the blood of Jesus, I destroy every witchcraft spirit in my life, in the name of Jesus.

Contradicting forces promoting hindrance in my life, die, in Jesus' name.

Every inspiration of witchcraft in my family, be destroyed, in the name of Jesus.

Blood of Jesus, blot out every evil mark of witchcraft in my life, in the name of Jesus.

Every garment put upon me by witchcraft, be torn to pieces, in the name of Jesus.

Angels of God, begin to pursue my household enemies, let their ways be dark and slippery, in the name of Jesus.

Lord, confuse them and turn them against themselves.

By the blood of Jesus, I break every evil unconscious agreement with household enemies concerning my miracles, in the name of Jesus.

Household witchcraft, fall down and die, in the name of Jesus.

Father Lord, drag all the household wickedness to the Dead Sea and bury them there.

Father Lord, I reject to follow the evil pattern of remote control my household enemies.

My life, jump out from the cage of household wickedness, in the name of Jesus.

I command all my blessings and potentials buried by wicked household enemies to be exhumed, in the name of Jesus.

I will see the goodness of the Lord in the land of the living, in the name of Jesus.

Everything done against me to spoil my joy, receive destruction, in the name of Jesus.

Father Lord, as Abraham received favor in Your eyes, let me receive Your favor, so that I can excel in every area of my life.

Lord Jesus, help my shortcoming and infirmities in the name of Jesus.

It does not matter, whether I deserve it or not, I receive immeasurable favor from the Lord, in the name of Jesus.

By the blood of Jesus I receive every blessing God has apportioned to me in the name of Jesus.

My blessing will not be transferred to my neighbor in the name of Jesus.

Father Lord, disgrace every power that is tormenting my breakthrough in the name of Jesus.

Every step I take shall lead to outstanding success, in Jesus' name.

I shall prevail with man and with God in every area of my life, in the name of Jesus.

Every habitation of infirmity in my life, break to pieces, in the name of Jesus.

My body, soul and spirit, reject every evil load, in Jesus' name.

Evil foundation in my life, I pull you down today, in the mighty name of Jesus.

Every inherited sickness in my life, depart from me now, in the name of Jesus.

Every evil water in my body, get out, in the name of Jesus.

By the blood of Jesus, I cancel the effect of every evil dedication in my life, in the name of Jesus.

Holy Ghost fire, immunize my blood against satanic poisoning, in the name of Jesus.

Father Lord, put self control in my mouth, in the name of Jesus.

I refuse to get accustomed to sickness, in the name of Jesus.

Every door open to infirmity in my life, be permanently closed today, in the name of Jesus.

Every power contenting with God in my life, be roasted, in the name of Jesus.

Every power preventing God's glory from manifesting in my life, be paralysed, in the name of Jesus.

I loose myself from the spirit of desolation, in the name of Jesus.

Father Lord break me through in my home, in the name of Jesus.

Father Lord keep in me healthy, in the name of Jesus.

Father Lord break me through in my business, in the name of Jesus.

Let God be God in my economy, in the name of Jesus.

Glory of God, envelope every department of my life, in the name of Jesus.

The Lord that answereth by fire, be my God, in the name of Jesus.

By the blood of Jesus, all my enemies shall scatter to rise no more, in the name of Jesus.

Blood of Jesus, cry against all evil gatherings arranged for my sake, in the name of Jesus.

Father Lord, convert all my past failures to unlimited victories, in the name of Jesus.

Lord Jesus, create room for my advancement in every area of my life.

All evil thoughts against me, Lord turn them to be good for me.

Father Lord, destroy anyone that is against my life in the name of Jesus.

Father Lord, advertise Your dumbfounding prosperity in my life.

Let the showers of dumbfounding prosperity fall in every department of my life, in the name of Jesus.

By the blood of Jesus, I claim all my prosperity in the name of Jesus.

Every door of my prosperity that has been shut, be opened now, in the name of Jesus.

Father Lord, convert my poverty to prosperity, in the name of Jesus.

Father Lord, convert my mistake to perfection, in the name of Jesus.

Father Lord, convert my frustration to fulfillment, in the name of Jesus.

Father Lord, bring honey out of the rock for me, in the name of Jesus.

By the blood of Jesus, I stand against every evil covenant of sudden death, in the name of Jesus.

By the blood of Jesus, I break every conscious and unconscious evil covenant of untimely death, in the name of Jesus.

You spirit of death and hell, you have no document in my life, in the name of Jesus.

You stones of death, depart from my ways, in the name of Jesus.

Father Lord, make me a voice of deliverance and blessing.

By the blood of Jesus, I tread upon the high places of the enemies, in the name of Jesus.

I bind and render useless, every blood sucking demon, in the name of Jesus.

You evil current of death, loose your grip over my life, in the name of Jesus.

By the blood of Jesus, I frustrate the decisions of the evil openers in my family, in the name of Jesus.

Fire of protection, cover my family, in the name of Jesus.

Father Lord, make my way perfect, in the name of Jesus.

Throughout the days of my life, I shall not be put to shame, in the name of Jesus.

By the blood of Jesus, I reject every garment of shame, in the name of Jesus.

By the blood of Jesus, I reject every shoe of shame, in the name of Jesus.

By the blood of Jesus, I reject every head-gear and cap of shame, in the name of Jesus.

Shamefulness shall not be my lot, in the name of Jesus.

Every demonic limitation of my progress as a result of shame, be removed, in the name of Jesus.

Every network of shame around me, be paralysed, in the name of Jesus.

Those who seek for my shame shall die for my sake, in the name of Jesus.

As far as shame is concerned, I shall not record any point for satan, in the name of Jesus.

In the name of Jesus, I shall not eat the bread of sorrow, I shall not eat the bread of shame and I shall not eat the bread of defeat.

No evil will touch me throughout my life, in the name of Jesus.

By the blood of Jesus, In every area of my life, my enemies will not catch me, in the name of Jesus.

By the blood of Jesus, In every area of my life, I shall run and not grow weary, I shall walk and shall not faint.

Father Lord, in every area of my life, let not my life disgrace You.

By the blood of Jesus, I will not be a victim of failure and I shall not bite my finger for any reason, in the name of Jesus.

Holy Spirit of God, Help me O Lord, to meet up with God's standard for my life.

By the blood of Jesus, I refuse to be a candidate to the spirit of amputation, in the name of Jesus.

By the blood of Jesus, with each day of my life, I shall move to higher ground, in the name of Jesus.

Every spirit of shame set in motion against my life, I bind you, in the name of Jesus.

Every spirit competing with my breakthroughs, be chained, in the name of Jesus.

By the blood of Jesus, I bind every spirit of slavery, in the name of Jesus.

By the blood of Jesus, In every day of my life, I disgrace all my stubborn pursuers, in the name of Jesus.

By the blood of Jesus, I bind, every spirit of Herod, in the name of Jesus.

Every spirit challenging my God, be disgraced, in Jesus' name.

Every Red Sea before me, be parted, in the name of Jesus.

By the blood of Jesus, I command every spirit of bad ending to be bound in every area of my life, in the name of Jesus.

By the blood of Jesus, Every spirit of Saul, be disgraced in my life, in the name of Jesus.

By the blood of Jesus, Every spirit of Pharaoh, be disgraced in my life, in Jesus' name.

By the blood of Jesus, I reject every evil invitation to backwardness, in Jesus' name.

By the blood of Jesus, I command every stone of hindrance in my life to be rolled away, in the name of Jesus.

Father Lord, roll away every stone of poverty from my life, in the name Jesus.

Let every stone of infertility in my marriage be rolled away, in the name of Jesus.

Let every stone of non-achievement in my life be rolled away, in the name of Jesus.

My God, roll away every stone of hardship and slavery from my life, in the name of Jesus.

My God, roll away every stone of failure planted in my life, my home and in my business, in the name of Jesus.

You stones of hindrance, planted at the edge of my breakthroughs, be rolled away, in the name of Jesus.

You stones of stagnancy, stationed at the border of my life, be rolled away, in the name of Jesus.

Father Lord, I thank You for all the stones You have rolled away, I forbid their return, in the name of Jesus.

Let the power from above come upon me, in the name of Jesus.

Father Lord, advertise Your power in every area of my life, in the name of Jesus.

Father Lord, make me a power generator, throughout the days of my life, in the name of Jesus.

Let the power to live a holy life throughout the days of my life fall upon me, in the name of Jesus.

Let the power to live a victorious life throughout the days of my life fall upon me, in the name of Jesus.

Let the power to prosper throughout the days of my life fall upon me, in the name of Jesus.

Let the power to be in good health throughout the days of my life fall upon me, in the name of Jesus.

Let the power to disgrace my enemies throughout the days of my life fall upon me, in the name of Jesus.

Let the power of Christ rest upon me now, in the name of Jesus.

Let the power to bind and loose fall upon me now, in the name of Jesus.

Father Lord, let Your key of revival unlock every department of my life for Your revival fire, in the name of Jesus.

Every area of my life that is at the point of death, receive the touch of revival, in the name of Jesus.

Father Lord, send down Your fire and anointing into my life, in the name of Jesus.

Every uncrucified area in my life, receive the touch of fire and be crucified, in the name of Jesus.

Let the fire fall and consume all hindrances to my advancement, in the name of Jesus.

You stubborn problems in my life, receive the Holy Ghost dynamite, in the name of Jesus.

You carry-over miracle from my past, receive the touch of fire in the name of Jesus.

Holy Ghost fire, baptize me with prayer miracle, in Jesus' name.

By the blood of Jesus, Every area of my life that needs deliverance, receive the touch of fire and be delivered, in the name of Jesus.

Let my angels of blessing locate me now, in the name of Jesus.

Every satanic programme of impossibility, I cancel you now, in the name of Jesus.

Every household wickedness and its programme of impossibility, be paralysed, in the name of Jesus.

No curse will land on my head, in the name of Jesus.

Throughout the days of my life, I will not waste money on my health: the Lord shall be my healer, in the name of Jesus.

Throughout the days of my life, I will be in the right place at the right time.

Throughout the days of my life, I will not depart from the fire of God's protection, in the name of Jesus.

Throughout the days of my life, I will not be a candidate for incurable disease, in the name of Jesus.

Every weapon of captivity, be disgraced, in the name of Jesus.

Let every attack planned against the progress of my life be frustrated, in the name of Jesus.

I command the spirits of harassment and torment to leave me, in the name of Jesus.

Lord, begin to speak soundness into my mind and being.

I reverse every witchcraft curse issued against my progress, in the name of Jesus.

I condemn all the spirits condemning me, in the name of Jesus.

Let divine accuracy come into my life and operations, in the name of Jesus.

No evil directive will manifest in my life, in the name of Jesus.

Let the plans and purposes of heaven be fulfilled in my life, in the name of Jesus.

O Lord, bring to me friends that reverence Your name and keep all others away.

Let divine strength come into my life, in the name of Jesus.

Let every stronghold working against my peace be destroyed, in the name of Jesus.

Let the power to destroy every decree of darkness operating in my life fall upon me now, in the name of Jesus.

Lord, deliver my tongue from evil silence.

Lord, let my tongue tell others of Your life.

Lord, loose my tongue and use it for Your glory.

Lord, let my tongue bring straying sheep back to the fold.

Lord, let my tongue strengthen those who are discouraged.

Lord, let my tongue guide the sad and the lonely.

Lord, baptise my tongue with love and fire.

Let every unrepentant and stubborn pursuers be disgraced in my life, in the name of Jesus.

Let every iron-like curse working against my life be broken by the blood of Jesus, in the name of Jesus.

Let every problem designed to disgrace me receive open shame, in the name of Jesus.

Let every problem anchor in my life be uprooted, in Jesus' name.

Multiple evil covenants, be broken by the blood of Jesus, in the name of Jesus.

Multiple curses, be broken by the blood of Jesus, in Jesus' name.

Everything done against me with evil padlocks, be nullified by the blood of Jesus, in the name of Jesus.

Everything done against me at any cross-roads, be nullified by the blood of Jesus, in the name of Jesus.

Let every stubborn and prayer resisting demon receive stones of fire and thunder, in the name of Jesus.

Every stubborn and prayer resisting sickness, loose your evil hold upon my life, in the name of Jesus.

Every problem associated with the dead, be smashed by the blood of Jesus, in the name of Jesus.

I recover my stolen property seven fold, in the name of Jesus.

Let every evil memory about me be erased by the blood of Jesus, in the name of Jesus.

By the blood of Jesus, I disallow my breakthroughs from being caged, in Jesus' name.

Let the sun of my prosperity arise and scatter every cloud of poverty, in the name of Jesus.

I decree unstoppable advancement upon my life, in Jesus' name.

I soak every day of my life in the blood of Jesus and in signs and wonders, in the name of Jesus.

I break every stronghold of oppression in my life, in Jesus' name.

Let every satanic joy about my life be terminated, in the name of Jesus.

I paralyze every household wickedness, in the name of Jesus.

Let every satanic spreading river dry up by the blood of Jesus, in the name of Jesus.

I bind every ancestral spirit and command them to loose their hold over my life, in the name of Jesus.

CONCLUSION

"And he changeth the times and the seasons: he removeth kings, and setteth up kings: he giveth wisdom unto the wise, and knowledge to them that know understanding." Daniel 2:21

For the most part, I do not know your personal trials and tribulation. But I am trusting the Lord that you will overcome this season of your life in the Mighty Name of Jesus.

It is written, "These things I have spoken unto you, that in me ye might have peace. In the world ye shall have tribulation: but be of good cheer; I have overcome the world." John 16:33

Life is practical and not mystical. Until we change our heart, we cannot change the outcome of our life. It is my heart desire that you make plans for eternity. Remember, *winner never quit and those who quit never win in life.*

If you are a born again Christian; we like to encourage you in your Christian life. If you are not a born again Christian we can help you here receive genuine salvation. *"Therefore if any man be in Christ, he is a new creature: old things are passed away; behold, all things are become new."* **2 Cor 5:17**

Now repeat this Prayer after me

Say Lord Jesus, I accept you today, as my Lord and my savior, forgive me of my sins wash me with your blood. Right now, I believe, I am sanctified, I am save, I am free, I am free from the Power of sin to serve the Lord Jesus. Thank you Lord for saving me. Amen.

Congratulations: You are now...

A BORN AGAIN CHRISTIAN.
Again I say to you—

CONGRATULATIONS!

What must I do to determine my divine visitation?

To determine divine visitation you must be born again! The word says as many as received him, to them gave He power to become the sons of God. Even to them that believe on his name.

To qualify for divine visitation, do the following with sincerity—

1) Acknowledge that you are a sinner and that He died for you. (Romans 3:23)

2) Repent of your sins. (Acts 3:19, Luke 13:5, 2 Peter 3:9)

3) Believe in your heart that Jesus died for your sin. (Romans 10:10)

4) Confess Jesus as the Lord over your life. (Romans 10:10, Acts 2:21)

Now repeat this Prayer after me

Say Lord Jesus, I accept you today, as my Lord and my savior, forgive me of my sins wash me with your blood. Right now, I believe, I am sanctified, I am save, I am free, I am free from the Power of sin to serve the Lord Jesus. Thank you Lord for saving me. Amen.

Congratulations: You are now...

A BORN AGAIN CHRISTIAN.
Again I say to you—

CONGRATULATIONS!

I adjure you to watch the Spirit of God bear witness with your Spirit confirming His word with signs following. The word says The Spirit itself beareth witness with our spirit, that we are the children of God. Join a bible believing church or join us on our weekly and Sunday worship services at 343 Sanford Avenue, Newark, New Jersey, 07106.

WISDOM KEYS

— Every Productive Society is a society heading to the top.

— Millions of Nigerians run away from Nigeria, very few Nigerians stay in Nigeria.

— My decision to return Nigeria is the will of God for my life.

— My short coming in America after 18 years, trained me to be wise, to think, reflect and reason appropriately.

— If you train your mind to reason it will train your hands to earn money.

— It is absurd to use the money of the heathen to build the kingdom of the living God.

— Every Ministry reveals its agenda and goal either at the beginning or at the end. Be careful of your life it is your first Ministry.

— The average American mind is conditioned for a continual quest to get new things and (discard the former) and throw away old things.

— When I considered well, my BMW jeep became my initial deposit for the work of the ministry in Nigeria.

— Money will never fall from any tree.

— Everyone is waiting for you to change your mind until you change your thinking nothing changes around you.

— Multiple academic degrees in other discipline gave me the chance to think, reflect and reason.

— What so everyone are thinking and reflecting at the moment reveals you to the time and the now factor .

—All events and intents are the product of precise thought processes, accurate reason every event is designed for a designated timeline.

— Wisdom is your ability to think, to create and invent. If you can think wise enough you will come out of penury.

— The distance between you and success is your creative ability to think reason and reflect accurate.

— Success is the result of hard work, commitment resolve and determination learning from past mistakes and failing.

— If you organize your mind you have organized your life and destiny.

— There is a thin line between success and failure. If you look above and beyond you are on your way to success.

— Wealth is your ability to think, power is your ability to reason and success is your ability to be informed.

— If you can make use of your mind by thinking and reasoning God will make use of your life and destiny.

— Think and Be Great.

— Reflect, Reason, Think and Be Great.

— Famous people are born of woman.

— That you will make it is your intention; that you will survive is your resolve, that you will succeed with changes is your determination, personal efforts and hard work.

— No man was born a failure. Lack of vision is the end product of failure.

— Working with mental patients encourages and aspire me to be a productive observant and dedicated to my assignment.

— Successful people are not magicians, it is the will power combined with hard work, and determination and a resolve to succeed that make them succeed.

— In the unequivocal state of the mind, intention is not a location or a position it is the state of the mind.

— So many people think, that they think. The mind is used to think, reflect, and reason. You will remain blind with your eye open until you can see with your mind by thinking.

— There is no favoritism in accurate and precise calculation.

— Although knowledge is power, information is the key and gateway to a great future.

— It will take the hand of God to move the hand of man.

— With the backing of the great wise God, nothing will disconnect you from your inheritance.

— As long as you have wisdom and understanding of God, Satan and evil cannot manipulate your life and destiny.

— You have come this far by yourself judgment and decision you have made in the past, now lean and listen to God for another dimension of greatness.

— Great people are common people it is extra ordinary effort and the price of sacrifice that produces greatness.

— As a mental direct care worker I saw a great pastor and a motivational speaker within myself.

— Menial job does not reduce your self-worth, until you resolve to achieve greatness see greatness in all you do; you will never count in your community.

— The principle of Jesus will solve your gambling and addiction problems.

— Everyone have their self-appraisal and what they think about you. Until you discover yourself other opinion about you will alter the real you.

— Supervisors and directors are just a position in the chain of command in a work place. Never allow your supervisor hierarchy to alter your opinion about yourself.

— Everyone can come out of debt if they make up their mind.

— That I am not a decision maker at work does not diminish my contribution to my world.

— Although it appears like it was a poor decision to accept a direct care employment at a psychiatric hospital as I reflect of my nine years of experience, it became apparent that I have learnt and experienced enough for my next assignment in life.

— Self-encouragement and determination is a resolve of the heart.

— If you are determined to make a difference, and do the things that make a difference you will eventually make a difference.

— Good things do not come easy.

— Short cuts will cut your life short.

— Those who look ahead move ahead.

— Life is all about making an impact. In your life time strive to make an impact in your community.

— Make friends and connect with people who are moving ahead of you in life.

— If you can look around well you have come a long way in your life, made a lot of difference and realized a lot of success in life.

— If you are my old friend, hurry up to reach out to me before I become a stranger to you.

— Everything I am blessed with inspirations from God, that change my definition and interpretation of the world around me.

— I thought I was stagnant and lonely until I looked around and noticed my children running around and my wife cooking.

— At 40 I resigned my Job to seek the Lord forever.

— My ministry took a drastic rise to the top when the wisdom of God visited me with knowledge and understanding.

— You will be a better person, if you understand the characteristics of your personality – your mood swings, attitudes, and habits.

— It is the seed of love you sow into the heart of a child and a woman that you reap in due time.

— Love is not selfish, love share everything including the concealed secrets of the mind.

— As long as you have a prayer life and a bible; you will never feel lonely, rejected, and idle in the race of life.

— When good friends disconnect from you, let them go, they might have seen something new in a different direction.

— Confidence in yourself and in God is the only way to bring you out of captivity.

— Never train a child to waste his/her time.

— The mind is the greatest assets of a great future.

— You walk by common sense run by principles and fly by instruction.

— Those who fly in flight of life fly alone.

— Up in the air you are alone. No one can toll you accept the compass of knowledge and information.

— I have seen a towing vehicle I have seen a towing ship I have never seen a tolling airplane.

— I exercise my judgment and make a decision every minute of the day.

— Decisions are crucial, critical and vital with reference to your future.

— So many people wish for a great future. You can only work towards a great future.

— Your celebrity status began when you discovered your talent. What are you good at? Work at it with all commitment.

— Prayers will sustain you but the wisdom of God will prosper you.

— When I met Oyedepo, his teachings changed my perspective. But when I met Ibiyeomie; His teaching changed my perception.

— I will be successful in ministry if only I concentrate and focus my energy in the work of the ministry.

— It took the late Dr. Vincent Pearle Norman's book to open my mind towards kingdom success.

CHAPTER 3

PRAYER OF SALVATION

"Neither is there salvation in any other: for there is none other name under heaven given among men, whereby we must be saved."
Acts 4:12

What must I do to determine my divine visitation?

To be saved we must be born again! The word says as many as received him, to them gave He power to become the sons of God. Even to them that believe on his name.

To qualify for divine visitation, do the following with sincerity—

1) Acknowledge that you are a sinner and that He died for you. (Romans 3:23)

2) Repent of your sins. (Acts 3:19, Luke 13:5, 2 Peter 3:9)

3) Believe in your heart that Jesus died for your sin. (Romans 10:10)

4) Confess Jesus as the Lord over your life. (Romans 10:10, Acts 2:21)

Now repeat this Prayer after me

Say Lord Jesus, I accept you today, as my Lord and my savior, forgive me of my sins wash me with your blood. Right now, I believe, I am sanctified, I am save, I am free, I am free from the Power of sin to serve the Lord Jesus. Thank you Lord for saving me. Amen.

Congratulations: You are now...

A BORN AGAIN CHRISTIAN.
Again I say to you—

CONGRATULATIONS!

I adjure you to watch the Spirit of God bear witness with your Spirit confirming His word with signs following. The word says The Spirit itself beareth witness with our spirit, that we are the children of God.

MIRACLE CARE OUTREACH

"...But that the members should have the same care one for another"
1 Corinthians 12:25

We are all members of the body of Christ. Jesus commanded us to love our neighbor as ourselves. This includes caring for one another as a member of one body. True love is expressed in caring and giving. The word says for God so Love He gave….

Reach out to someone in need of Jesus, help someone in crisis find Christ. Look out and prove your love to Jesus by caring and inviting your friends and associates to find Jesus the Healer.

Invite your friends to our Home Care Cell Fellowship (Miracle chapel Intl Satellite fellowship) In the USA at 33 Schley Street, Newark, New Jersey, 07112. Home Care Cell fellowship Group meets every Tuesday at 6:00pm-7:00pm.

If you are in Nigeria—**MIRACLE OF GOD MINISTRIES**, aka **"MIRACLE CHAPEL INTL"** Mpama –Egbu-Owerri Imo state Nigeria.

Chapter 3   Prayer of Salvation

LIFE IS NOT ALL ABOUT DURATION— BUT ITS ALL ABOUT DONATION

What does the above statement mean?....

Life consists not in the accumulation of material wealth. (Luke 12:15) But it's all about liberality...meaning - what you can give and share with others. Proverb11:25. When you live for others—You live forever - because you out live your generation by the legacy you live behind after you depart into glory to be with the Lord. But when you live to yourself - you are reduced to self—you are easily forgotten when you die and depart in glory. Permit me to admonish you today to live your life to be a blessing to a soul connected to you today. I want you to know that so many souls are connected and looking up to you, and through you so many souls will be saved and rescued from destruction. Will you disciple someone today to find Jesus Christ?

As a genuine Christian; it is your duty to evangelize Jesus Christ to all you meet on your way. Jesus is still in the healing business-Jesus is still doing miracles from time of old to now. Therefore tell someone about Jesus Christ today, disciple and bring them to Church. (John 1:45) Philip findeth Nathanael....

Please to prove the sincerity of your love

for God today; please become a soul winner. The dignity of your Christianity is hidden in your boldness to proclaim and evangelize Jesus Christ to all you meet on your way. There is a question mark on the integrity of your Christianity until you become a life soul winner. Invite someone to join us worship the Lord Jesus this coming Sunday. Amen.

MIRACLE OF GOD MINISTRIES

PILLARS OF THE COMMISSION

We Believe Preach and Practice the following:

1) We believe and preach Salvation to every living human being

2) We believe and preach Repentance and forgiveness of sins

3) We believe and preach the baptism of the Holy Spirit and Spiritual gifts

4) We believe and teach the Prosperity

5) We believe and preach Divine Healing and Miracles (Signs & Wonder)

6) We believe and preach Faith

7) We believe and proclaim the Power of God (Supernatural)

8) We believe and proclaim Praise & Worship to God

9) We believe and preach Wisdom

10) We believe and preach Holiness (Consecration)

11) We believe and preach Vision

12) We believe and teach the Word of God

13) We believe and teach Success

14) We believe and practice Prayer

15) We believe and teach Deliverance

These 15 stones form the Pillars of Our Commission. Become part of this church family and follow this great move of God.

MY HEART FELT PRAYER FOR YOU

It is my desire as a pastor, to hear of your testimonies. I feel fulfilled every time I hear of your testimony. Therefore take a few minutes and write me, if you please Miracle of God Ministries 33 Schley Street, Newark, New Jersey, 07112.

Now let me pray for you:

Lord Jesus, I give you thanks especially for this precious one reading this small book. Father change their lives and circumstances in the mighty Name of Jesus. Heal everyone that is sick, and deliver the captive, In Jesus Mighty Name. Amen.

SEEK THE FACE OF THE LORD IN PRAYERS

We must always seek the face of the Lord in prayer, especially in time of predicaments, and prevailing challenges in life. As long as we live changes are inevitable.

We must always seek the face of the Lord in prayer, in intercession and in thanksgiving. Anyone without a prayer life has no for God. We encounter God in prayers. Every time we pray we meet with God. I encourage you to continue seeking the face of the Lord in prayers, in thanksgiving and in intercession. Prayer is so important to the Lord Jesus that He taught His apostles how to pray.

"And it came to pass, that, as he was praying in a certain place, when he ceased, one of his disciples said unto him, Lord, teach us to pray, as John also taught his disciples.

And he said unto them, When ye pray, say, Our Father which art in heaven, Hallowed be thy name. Thy kingdom come. Thy will be done, as in heaven, so in earth.

Give us day by day our daily bread.

And forgive us our sins; for we also forgive every one that is indebted to us. And lead us not into temptation; but deliver us from evil."
Luke 11:1-4

CHAPTER 4
ABOUT THE AUTHOR

Rev Franklin N Abazie is the founding and Presiding Pastor of Miracle of God Ministries with headquarters in Newark, New Jersey USA and a branch church in Owerri- Imo State Nigeria. He is following the footsteps of one of his mentors, Oral Roberts (Healing Evangelist) of the blessed memory. The Lord passed Oral Roberts healing mantle two days before he went to be with the Lord at age 91 into the hand of healing evangelist-Rev Franklin N Abazie in a vision.

In all his services the Power and Presence of God is present to heal all in his audience. He is an ordained man of God with a Healing Ministry reviving the healing and miracle ministry of Jesus Christ of Nazareth.

Pastor Franklin N Abazie, is called by God with a unique mandate: **"THE MOMENT IS DUE TO IMPACT YOUR WORLD THROUGH THE REVIVAL OF THE HEALING & MIRACLE MINISTRY OF JESUS CHRIST OF NAZARETH**

"I AM SENDING YOU TO RESTORE HEALTH UNTO THEE AND I WILL HEAL

THEE OF THY WOUNDS. SAID THE LORD OF HOST"

Rev. Abazie is a gifted ardent Teacher of the word of God who operates also in the office of a Prophet, generating and attracting undeniable signs & wonders, special miracles and healings, with apostolic fireworks of the Holy Ghost. He is the founding and presiding senior Pastor of this fast growing Healing ministry. He has written over 86 inspirational, healing and transforming books covering almost all aspect of divine healing and life. He is happily married and blessed with children.

BOOKS BY REV FRANKLIN N ABAZIE

1) *The Outcome of Faith*
2) *Understanding the secret of prevailing Prayers*
3) *Commanding Abundance*
4) *Understanding the secret of the man God uses*
5) *Activating my due Season*
6) *Overcoming Divine Verdicts*
7) *The Outcome of Divine Wisdom*
8) *Understanding God's Restoration Mandate*
9) *Walking in the Victory and Authority of the truth*
10) *Gods Covenant Exemption*
11) *Destiny Restoration Pillars*
12) *Provoking Acceptable Praise*
13) *Understanding Divine Judgment*
14) *Activating Angelic Re-enforcement*
15) *Provoking Un-Merited Favor*
16) *The Benefits of the Speaking faith*
17) *Understanding Divine Arrangement*
18) *Put your faith to work*
19) *Developing a positive attitude in life*
20) *The Power of Prevailing faith*
21) *Inexplicable faith*
22) *The intellectual components of Redemption.*
23) *Dominating Controlling Spirit*
24) *Understanding Divine Prosperity*
25) *Understanding the secret of the man God Uses*
26) *Retaining Your Inheritance*
27) *Never give up hope*
28) *Commanding Angelic Escorts*
29) *The winner's faith*
30) *Understanding Your Guardian Angels*
31) *Overcoming the Dominion of Sin*
32) *Understanding the Voice of God*

33) The Outstanding benefits of the Anointing
34) The Audacity of the Blood of Jesus
35) Walking in the Reality of the Anointing
36) The Mystery of Divine supply
37) Understanding Your Harvest Season
38) Activating Your Success Buttons
39) Overcoming the forces of Darkness
40) Overcoming the devices of the devil
41) Overcoming Demonic agents
42) Overcoming the sorrows of failure
43) Rejecting the Sorrows of failure
44) Resisting the Sorrows of Poverty
45) The Restoring broken Marriages.
46) Redeeming Your Days
47) The force of Vision
48) Overcoming the forces of ignorance
49) Understanding the sacrifice of small beginning
50) The might of small beginning
51) Praying in the Spirit
52) Dominating controlling Spirits
53) Breaking the shackles of the curse of the law
54) Covenant keys to answered prayers
55) Wisdom for Signs & Wonders
56) Wisdom for generational Impact
57) Wisdom for Marriage Stability
58) Understanding the number of your Days
59) Enforcing Your Kingdom Rights
60) Escaping the traps of immoralities
61) Escaping the trap of Poverty
62) Accessing Biblical Prosperity
63) Accessing True Riches in Christ
64) Silencing the Voice of the Accuser
65) Overcoming the forces of oppositions
66) Quenching the voice of the avenger
67) Silencing demonic Prediction & Projection
68) Silencing Your Mocker

69) Understanding the Power of the Holy Ghost
70) Understanding the baptism of Power
71) The Mystery of the Blood of Jesus
72) Understanding the Mystery of Sanctification
73) Understanding the Power of Holiness
74) Praying in the spirit
75) Activating the Forces of Vengeance
76) Appreciating the Mystery of Restoration
77) Covenant Keys to Answered Prayers
78) Engaging the mystery of the blood
79) Commanding the Power of the Speaking faith
80) Uprooting the forces against Your Rising
81) Overcoming mere success syndrome
82) Understanding Divine Sentence
83) Understanding the Mystery of Praise
84) Understanding the Author of Faith
85) The Mystery of the finisher of faith
86) Where is your trust?

MIRACLE OF GOD MINISTRIES

*NIGERIA CRUSADE
2012*

MIRACLE OF GOD MINISTRIES

NIGERIA CRUSADE 2012

MIRACLE OF GOD MINISTRIES

NIGERIA CRUSADE 2012

www.ingramcontent.com/pod-product-compliance
Lightning Source LLC
Chambersburg PA
CBHW021133300426
44113CB00006B/408